"You don't read an Ed Tato poem, you experience it. First and foremost a storyteller, Tato traverses, sticks and weaves through working-class milieus that include hotels and factories and the man of the desolate places most people would never care to glimpse with surrealistic imagery that combines a hard-hitting reality. Part Eliot, part-Simic with some Bukowski—although don't bank on the typical Buk tropes—Tato is an original on his own. *Dead Ends, Detours, Blinds Curves and Roundabout Road Home* is unlike anything you've read and well-worth the investment."

-Nathan Graziano, author of *Fly Like The Seagull*

"Tato's poems are a revelation. They move patiently and with great assurance past personal landmarks, through soft despair, through quiet strength, through resignation, and then come out on the other end with a unique sense of unsettled certainty. These are poems that believe in the power of mystery, that embody the concept of quiet strength. They drift, but never waver. They soar, but remain grounded. Most importantly, as we all spiral down deeper and deeper into the abyss of petty grievances and tribal mindsets that the modern world has become, these are poems that offer no appeasement, only the stark beauty of unvarnished, unapologetic truth."

-John Sweet, author of *A Dead Man, Either Way*

"More bout than book, this collection from Ed Tato puts you in the ring with a Brink's driver, a barber and hunchback from Humboldt (hometown of Walter Johnson). You'll hit the circuit from Pittsburgh to Buffalo, from Lawrence to Wabash in these stick and move poems that never go for the knockout but jab, jab jab. And you've got the cornerman in Tato to make it to the bell. Porkpie and chewed-ended stogie and towel rolled in his right hand. Ice and andreline. Keep the jab, he says, find the footwork and when one lands stay with it for a beat. Feel it. And what you learn here is that there is nothing more, there is just this. A rickety stool, the sweatsmell and the sting of wanting it to be more than a match. Gloves up."

-Jason Wesco, author of *Rough Traces*

"Tato is a details man and a blues man, the kind of storyteller you're afraid to invite over unless you want to relive your most harrowing adventures through his sharp, sorrowful, if not compassionate eyes. These poems ignite all five senses, bringing the reader to life: missing people they've never met before, hearing highways heave in cityscapes they've never even visited, suddenly craving Player's Navy Cut cigarettes. This book is full of tales from the front -- of a life clearly spent living -- and wisdom rooted in spirited, but humble experience."

-Timothy Tarkelly, author of *On Slip Rigs and Spiritual Growth* (OAC Books) and *Luckhound* (Spartan Press).

Dead Ends, Detours, Blind Curves and a Roundabout Road Home

Poems by Ed Tato

Spartan Press

Spartan Press
Kansas City, MO
spartanpress.com

Copyright © Ed Tato, 2021
First edition 1 3 5 7 9 10 8 6 4 2
ISBN: 978-1-952411-37-3
LCCN: 2020951607

Cover image and author photo: Elizabeth Kneebone.
All rights reserved. No part of this publication may be
reproduced or transmitted in any form or by any means,
electronic or mechanical, including photocopying,
recording or by info retrieval system, without prior
written permission from the author.

I am especially grateful to Michael Steven and Kilmog Press in New Zealand, who published the poems in "A Roundabout Road Home" as the limited edition hand-bound chapbook, "Red Sky Blues."

Thanks also to the publications who first printed a version of these poems:

I70 Review	"Absolute Humidity"
Nthposition	"Ground Clutter"
Full of Crow	"Wet Bulb Depression"
Curbside Splendor	"Radial Velocity"
Belleville Park Pages	"Downburst"
Two Hawks Quarterly	"U Burst"
Present Magazine	"Those Who Stay," "Those Who Return"
Monday Night	"Mackerel Sky," "Quality of Snow"

And finally, thank you to the Kansas poets who made these better poems.

Jason Wesco
Jackie Treiber
Jason Ryberg
Sarah Ruhlen
Will Leathem
Mark Hennessy
Chris Citro
Mickey Cesar

-ET

TABLE OF CONTENTS

Working Maintenance at the Senator Chapman
   Estates and Other Rundown Joints in Syracuse,
  New York / 1

You Bend / 5

He's a Monkey / 8

Fructus Naturales / 21

Delaware and Delavan / 25

Hunchbacks / 34

Those Who Go / 45

Those Who Stay / 50

Those Left Behind / 54

Those Who Return / 57

Those Who Arrive / 62

The Farewells / 66

Absolute Humidity / 77

Backscatter / 79

Cyclogenesis / 81

Downburst / 83

Exit Region / 84

Friction / 86

Ground Clutter / 88

Heat Index / 89

Instability / 91

January Thaw / 95

K Index / 97

Latent Heat / 99

Mackerel Sky / 101

Nephelococcygia / 104

Occluded Front / 108

Prefrontal Trough / 110

Quality of Snow / 112

Radial Velocity / 114

Sun Dog / 118

Towering Cumulus / 121

U Burst / 124

Virga / 126

Wet Bulb Depression / 128

X-Rays / 130

Yellow Wind / 133

Zastrugi / 136

DEAD ENDS

*Struck me kinda funny, funny yea indeed,
how at the end of every hard earned day
you can find some reason to believe*

>   -Bruce Springteen,
>   "Reason to Believe"

Working Maintenance at the Senator Chapman Estates and Other Rundown Joints in Syracuse, New York

I hear squawking crows
fly east to feed
as Venus flickers through an inky sky
that might, if black clouds break,
turn sky blue.

Icicles roost in eaves,
perched above a woman who's
dropped a rolled Post-Standard behind a storm door,
and now, in a snug-fitting skirt,
crowhops off the icepacked porch
doing her best not to notice I notice.

Three gunshots.
Four more burst back.

Columbus and Fayette —
a few blocks up.

No random gunplay that,
and no need to hurry home.

The jet-stream bites through cracked boots crunching over snow.

Keys jangle then catch in a lock.
I wipe my eyes and nose.
Sirens wail at last.

I am cold all over.

Something,
that might or might not be
water, pools in the ceiling above my toilet,
drips into my tub
and stains my towel and mat.

The tenant upstairs answers only after I bash
with the butt end of a sixteen inch pipe wrench
his cracked rattling door.

That guy at the Eddie James,
who's toilet was clogged, he'd said,
since the day he'd moved in,
couldn't even manage that.
Three weeks is what he'd said,
and his bowl was full —
packed-in-mounded-above-the-rim-what-the-fuck-full —

but when I got back with the tools
he lay on his back on the bed,
on the nod, croaking
something half wheeze, half retch —
a played-out needle and Police Gazette beside him.

And now this Joe No One
grips a threadbare towel stretched around his gut.
Droplets flicker on chicken-skin flesh.
He rubs his eyes and sniffles.
I can't tell if he's thirty or fifty-five,
but he sure seems afraid.
Most of them do.

I shove in.
I hear the shower sputter.
A mattress and box spring crammed
foot to foot
crowd the one-room flat.

A woman, prone on the mattress,
head propped against the wall,
swears she's his mother —
her beak tells me this is true.
She does not look at me,
or away from the television.

She claws a magazine to the floor.
A man on TV — barely audible
above a crackling police scanner —
tells us all how, *Shots rang out
in the early morning dawn.*

Mom clutches her skirt,
bares a scaly thigh
and squawks at the box.

Animals
is what she says.

You Bend

Grout bags bang around the corner
open and upright on their conveyor belt.

60-pound bags.
80-pound bags.

The belt turns again
and drops acutely.
The bags turn and drop, acutely also,
then plummet from belt to floor
in a cloud of grout dust.

You bend and roll the top of the bag;
you grab the roll;
you bend and lift the bag —
not with a save-your-back lift,
not from the knees, frogman style —
you lift with your back.
Anything else is too slow, too clumsy.

You lift the bag and shake it once,
just enough to get the grout to settle,
just enough to cause another grout cloud.

You unroll the top of the bag
and pull out the flaps at each end;
you open the slits on the sides of each bag
and stuff the flaps into the slits
then heave the bag onto a pallet —
nine 60-pound bags per layer,
seven layers per pallet;
six 80-pound bags per layer,
eight layers per pallet.

Then you do it all again
only faster,

because the man filling the bags gets paid by the bag
and you get paid by the hour,
because a bag coming down the conveyor belt that rams
another bag
topples both bags
and spills the grout and costs the company money
and makes a bigger grout cloud,

and when you fill a pallet —
with 63 bags, with 48 bags —
you grab your shrink-wrap and sprint around that pallet
and whistle for the man on the forklift,

who, you hope, moves the full pallet out
and gets an empty one back
before the next bag arrives,

because the conveyor belt runs
and the bags are going to collide
and the foreman needs his fix —
and you don't really care for the taste of grout dust.

And the conveyor belt runs.
It runs from 2 a.m. until 4 a.m.
and you smoke for fifteen minutes,
then it runs from 4:15 until 6:15
and you swallow some food
and smoke as many smokes as you can smoke,
then it runs from 6:45 until 8:45
and you smoke for fifteen minutes,
then it runs from 9 until 11
and you smoke for fifteen minutes,

then it runs from 11:15 until 1:15 —
and all you want
is to keep the grout dust down.

He's a Monkey

So I'm at the front desk
because there are sixty-three rooms of Patels
and who-knows-how-many black bags
labelled or not labelled Patel.
There is, we know, one bell captain
who's too screwed to write shit down.

The Bigbys chat up the new desk clerk,
a blond I'd like to know when she not so frazzled.
I flash them all my Happy Bellman Smile.

I wait. I wave at Aloysius,
who sits on the counter — in a standard blue blazer,
shirt embroidered with all fifty states,
bow tie, knee pants and propeller beanie.

The clerk starts fawning over Aloysius,
and you can see it coming,
big as a biblical omen flaming across the sky,
so I start shaking my head, and waving at her,
and my eyes, I'm sure, are jumping out their sockets,
but it's too late.

She done called him a pretty monkey.

Now you know what happens next.
The Mrs. gets all lathered up
with her, *He's no monkey!*
He's an ape — Hylobates lar —
white-handed gibbon.

Maybe.
But we all know
who the monkey is around here.

They fume off for high tea —
her, the husband, the pretty monkey.
High tea! Who takes a monkey to high tea?

I'm thinking, though,
good riddance to bad news,
time to get tight with Blondie.

No way, you say?
No way, indeed.

The harpist promenades by.
The manager taps me with her clipboard,
eyes fixed to the front door.

I lug who-knows-which Patel's bag back and trade it
for a balky harp case with a broke-dick wheel,
which I roll to high tea, greeting everyone I meet
with my Earnest Bellman Hello!

The harpist grazes my arm,
looks ever so deeply into my eyes.
I'm sure I spot a happy-sad-golly-gosh-thank-you-tear
welling up as if we'd just rescued a kitten from a tree,
which makes me glow, knowing I'd be a fool
to be in this for tips.

Mister Hugo snaps his fingers.
He needs the best gentleman's club in Phoenix,
but he'd rather not ask the desk clerk,
because, well, she's kinda cute
and he'd like to ask her out,
so she might think he's a creep,
and, then, he thinks he's maybe mentioned the wife,
but he can't be sure about that.
We walk out, and I sum them up and flag his limo.
He'll get me later, he says,
and I says,
What? Oh no. Go on!

The bell captain nabs me.
Patel? Is it done?

It is not,
and, apparently, not meant to be,
as a cab skids in at us,
doors and trunk akimbo,
and I scuttle away, as the driver — C. K. Patel —
one Patel I know for sure —
dumps everything across the drive
and scrams for his next fare.

The guy,
Dickie Finnister from Pittsburgh,
has, no shit, a suitcase the size of Montana,
a torn Hefty bag, and,
get this,
a bagpipe!

His reservation?
The Miles-Away-Ocotillo-Suite,
but you knew that.

Luckily, there's plenty to talk about,
like the weather,

here,
in Pittsburgh
and in every other town he's lived in or visited.

He sees the monkey munching a madeleine.
Ooh, what a pretty monkey.

I says, *That's Aloysius.*
He's no monkey!
He's an ape — Hylobates lar —
white-handed gibbon.

He bets the monkey loves the weather here.
Sure. Why not?
I mean, damn, who doesn't
love summertime in the desert?
And I paint a pretty picture, of Aloysius
sunbathing atop a cactus-lined papago,
or lolling with coyotes,
but Dickie's back in Dubuque
and Wabash and San Diego.

San Diego,
now that's a town for weather,
a little breezy, though.

He picks a couple of kumquats from the kumquat bush
which is actually a tree
or shrub,
just like the kumquat, *Citrus japonica*,
is actually fortunella as much as citrus.

My man tells me they're the best baby-oranges he's ever had —
better than Tampa, where they really know their oranges,
but it rains too much in winter.

I tell him they're kumquats.

He chomps on,
Pittsburgh,
95, this summer,
hotter than here.

I say, *Last week, 122.*

He gives me that look,
you know the one —
he says,
hell, he says the same thing they all say,
that bullshit about dry heat,
then he pops a kumquat in his gob,
smacks his lips and rolls his eyes at me.

Motherfucker.

Dickie can't believe his rooms
and the croquet pitch
and the mountain view
and the weather
and just look at those gardens
chock-full of baby-orange trees.
He envies me, boy, he really does!
Oh, how I must love it here, too.

I don't know how many Patel bags await
even as their owners and tips do not.
I know plenty of banter I could have dropped
on the cutie clerk whose name I still don't know.
And I know what I'd tell Dickie,
what we'd all say, if you could make a dime
being honest.

He digs in his pocket,
though, it turns out,
no surprise,
only for another kumquat.

He'd bet half my pay, he says,
kumquat juice dribbling down his chin,
that that pretty monkey just can't get enough baby-oranges.

True, says I,
but he's no monkey.

DETOURS

Cause it all come from the blue

       -John Lee Hooker
       "(You'll Never Amount to Anything If You
       Don't Go to) Collage (A Fortuitous
       Concatenation of Events)"

Fructus Naturales

You think you know
this song,
but no,
you're not really sure.
And, as for what passes
as conversation, you've heard
it all. Already. Frequently. Here,
at the Shot Time Bar and Grill,
or any other joint like it, in and around Wichita,
where noise gets served. So
you stare at the credit card reader,
as the barmaid's cat paws
yet again another squawking mouse,

because
the silence you crave
germinates before you, aflower,
you'd like to believe,
in pinpricks of greenish light.

An ache between
your kneecap and knee.

That would be the meniscus —
no matter what the doctors say —
and a symptom of age,
or the endless snap of sub-zero weather.
It might be each shift spent squatting
to harvest then bind clanking bundles of rebar,
or every night you pushed, and were pulled by,
a sputtering Viper Fang 18C floor scrubber
and every earlier iteration,
each of which leaked
from the same gasket
to swamp rotten boots
and cultivate the fungus
asprout between your toes.

It might be you —
fated for this bar-stool,
days and nights unyoked from chatter, drama
or any impulse toward human frailty.

Someone caterwauls for Spaceman Red,
and the barmaid flips him off
then pours you two more
and rolls her eyes and rings you up —

her left hand's velocity
like the hooker at Broadway and Osie.

Lefty,
also known as Spaceman —
a nickname bestowed to praise
his demeanor after prodigious bong-hits —
rode shotgun with you
for Brinks,
likewise
at Broadway and Osie.

Your side-arms stunk of oil,
as did the Remington
you'd groggily load and lock
and unload every day,
like that day —
the day
Lefty coaxed a kitten into the hold.

The radio's repeating refrain warrants no immanent end
to the tune you thought you knew,
only electrochemical impulses which pass for music
and forewarn an ear-worm in waiting,
whose monotony —

when it reappears, one day
weeks or months or years from this one,
as you beeswax your boots
or knock the mud from them,
thereby scraping a new tear in the knee's cartilage —
will bring you back here again,
to this pain,
and this barmaid,
to that same whore as always,
and then, evermore, to Lefty again,
though, you'd like to hope,
at some point, maybe
not to the kitten —
who you'd forgotten once —
until it squealed
clawing up your leg
a heartbeat before
the shotgun thunders.

Delaware and Delavan

Bus 26 is
out of sight, is
down the road and out of sight, and
Capra waits; waits
looking at his hands; waits.
His cuticles are chapped and cracked and
waiting, torn away from the nails with waiting.

Some blood, some
dried blood in one of the cracks of the cuticle,
a drop of blood,
a drop of dried brown blood dries
in a crack of a dried cracked cuticle.
That nail is split too,
that nail,
on the pinky finger.
The one on the left hand.

There's a metal shaving
lodged on the inside of the second knuckle
of the pointer finger on that same left hand.

That finger,
that same finger,
and the one beside it, is
brown,
tobacco tar smoked to the filter nicotine brown.
Those fingers,
those two fingers, those
brown fingers, rise to his nose;
he smells and he inhales and he
lights another Export.

The nail on the left thumb is blueblack and yellow purple green.

The metal shaving, the
shaving in the knuckle,
the second knuckle,
makes the knuckle red
and swollen, and
he sees there is some pus.
That shaving
cannot be pulled out
or scratched out,
won't be pinched out
of the knuckle of the hand,

that same hand that
stroked her wrist,
that held her hand
until she couldn't stand
his damp clammy sweating.

~

Ashes from the Export
fall, fall and are flicked from the Export,
and are flicked off the front of a
shirt, are flicked to the sidewalk,
are flicked and fall on shoes,
a loafer to the left,
an oxford on the right.

~

He sees a line of cars.
There is a line cars, a line of yellow cars,
a line of yellow cars gleaming in the sun, aflame in the sun,
coming from Main, crawling up Delavan.
He starts to count the cars
   five then ten then fifteen
because they all look the same,

    twenty-one twenty-two twenty-three
and now he sees the hearse out front,
    thirty-six thirty-seven
and these cars,
these yellow glinting cars,
are all taxi cabs,
    forty-nine
with a black flag
    fifty-five fifty-six
on each antenna,
    fifty-eight
and the black flags are funeral home flags.

Amigone Funeral Home flags.

~

He sees police tape,
again,
and a man with the notebook, again,
sirens and strobe lights again,
and this time he's in a cab
idling at a curb.

The cabby's head is covered by a cap,
a green and yellow cap,
a Green Bay Packers cap perhaps.

A cigarette rests
behind an ear,
the left one.

A flannel,
a tan green purple navy yellow flannel,
a plaid flannel above a
t-shirt has some tobacco,
some flakes and ashes,
some tobacco
spilled onto it.

Lizard,
Ball,
the words on the t-shirt beneath the flannel
are Lizard Ball;
there is something else
there, but there is
Lizard Ball.

A pack of
Players Navy Cut cigarettes
is in a pocket,
the left breast pocket
of the flannel over the Lizard Ball t-shirt.
Another cigarette,
one of the Players Navy Cut cigarettes,
an unsmoked unlit cigarette rests by a shoe,
a sneaker,
a black sneaker,
a black leather sneaker with three white stripes.
Adidas.

The Players Navy Cut cigarette rests
by a black and white Adidas
on the right foot
of the cabby;
the cigarette lingers,
like the shoe and its foot,
immobile between accelerator and brake.

A white sock,
above the right Adidas,
the black leather one with the three white stripes,
a white sock above this shoe and
below jeans,

green Levi's jeans, green
straight cut jeans,
jeans stained on the thighs,
by something brown,
jeans stained by chocolate maybe.

Below these jeans
and above that shoe,
the white sock
rests at an angle,
an angle that is the same angle
as that at which that cigarette lies —
the unsmoked unlit Players Navy Cut cigarette
that has fallen,
from somewhere,
to the floor of the cab,
that has fallen
from the pack in the pocket
of the flannel.

That flannel is
a flannel with one sleeve,
the left sleeve,
rolled up above the elbow,
the left elbow of the cabby in the cab.

The flannel is rolled above the elbow
and above a green and yellow bungee cord
tied tight about the arm
above the same left elbow.

The flannel is
rolled up above a needle,
a hypodermic needle,
stuck in the arm,
the same left arm with the rolled up flannel
and the wound up bungee cord.

The plunger of the needle
stuck in the arm
is plunged fully in,
but a drop of blood,
of brown looking blood,
has flooded back into the hub of the needle.

A spoon,
a souvenir spoon from Crystal Beach,
burnt black and blue on the bottom,
a souvenir spoon sits on the seat.
A Zippo lighter and some cotton,
a cotton ball,
sit next to the spoon

on the seat
in the cab —
the cab of the cabby in flannel —
a cab that stinks
of sulfur and vomit,
and vinegar,
just a whiff of vinegar —

the cab of the cabby who's dead,
who's in the hearse,
ahead of the cabs —
the fifty-eight cabs in front of the bus —
the bus that's meant to stop
in front of the cemetery,
the bus meant to pick Capra up
at Delaware and Delavan,
the bus that does not stop at the cemetery
after all the cabs
turn in —
a bus that never could
take him far enough away from here
or himself.

Hunchbacks
- After Charles Simic's *St. Thomas Aquinas*

I hide scraps of myself everywhere
for the down-and-out clods
who prospect gutters and alleys
for another man's trash
not the lucky few
who believe
themselves complete.

The day my father,
a railroad lifer
and missing bits aficionado,
turned sixty,
he gave the lawn mower,
to scatter across our yard,
his left big toe.

Today was someone else's
birthday, her forty-first birthday,
and I kept it quietly, disturbed
not at all by a nosefull of something
that wasn't what it was
meant to be

and only some by all
those things that weren't
what one thought
one meant
to find,

like a one-legged blue-jay
mounting its green jay mate,
or the guy in broken clogs
out behind the KFC
butchering some critter
whose hide glistens a deep purplish black.

He invited me to tea,
and I was tempted
by an oddly nasal bass-baritone
boasting about his nine-pine prowess
and Lionel train switching stations.

~

The birthday-girl and me
would roam where empty Kansas sky would have us go.

We found Walter "Big Train" Johnson's boyhood home
hidden somewhere among heat and dust and glittering
junk shops marooned in unremembered towns —
like Humboldt,
where a hunchbacked octogenarian brandished
a dubiously faint autograph. He said Big Train
wore a wool union suit to keep cool on days such as this,
said, road greys or home whites,
it didn't make a lick of difference,
though spiked iced-tea never hurt, neither.

My father regarded wool with likewise affection
and held forth often on its virtues
during our annual excursion to Sal Maglie Stadium —
so named for Sal "The Barber,"
our tribal home-town hero,
surpassed only, only to me, only some,
by Three-Finger Brown.

~

I've come back east alone,
where, I'd been told, my ancestors reckoned
hunchbacks — del gobbo — as fortuitous omens,
where summer was less tragically borne
because rivers, here, run blue, not brown or dry.

I ride my bike along the Niagara.
I stop at the Black Rock Canal crossing.
I always stop at the Black Rock Canal crossing, hoping
the International Railway Bridge swings its rusty trusses
ninety degrees across the channel,
clearing way for boats to pass.

Tonight, a wedding party cruises my way,
and the bridge rotates away through fog.
It rotates back. It crashes shut, jarring
me and the video my phone records for the girl.

I'd done the Italian language mass, for her,
Easter morning, as widows fingered rosary beads and wept.

~

I'm resurrected.
I'm a Saint, like Celsus, whose finger wouldn't burn,
I beamed to the dowager-humped Chick
at her almost empty Bar & Bowl,
where I'd dispatched several iced-teas and gin,
and bowled my first two-hundred game,
using the ball my father rubbed to a blueblack lapis gloss
then cradled daintily, before he spun it down the lane

certain its late hook
would rupture the pocket,
which brought his face a hint of smile —
like a smile missing its curve.

I find this same absence
in pictures of me as a boy.

The ball these days is nicked from when I dropped it.
The soles of his bowling shoes have cracked.
The tongues ripped out
from I don't remember why.

He owned a cabin
in some life that predates me.
He never spoke of it,
but I found a box of photos
after he died.
The bear in this photo is a blurred black shape
among grays and whites. It sags,
head-down, from a hook,
one foot at an odd obtuse angle.
There's no discernible sun.

A man, before he was my father, coiled
at his haunches, grips a knife.

I know where
the bear's nose and tongue and ears end up,
and I see that bear's look
on everyone I meet.

I would look away

if I believed
in venerable relics or hunchback charms —
if I could find anything other
than all the offal
left behind
once everything's been cleft.

BLIND CURVES

A tune beyond us as we are,
Yet nothing changed by the blue guitar

> -Wallace Stevens,
> "The Man with the Blue Guitar"

Those Who Go

Whitey, ever
the voice of reason,
pours kümmel over ice
as eyes rolling up in wagging head
indicate, yes, indeed, we have
had this conversation before.

I step off right quick
with six gypsies possessed
by a need to find and swim to
something called halfway rock.

At the Whirlpool bridge
ancient sounds, border guards
and creased C-notes
scuttle about.

Timo, or so the badge says,
bites a uniform cuff
while his other hand waves us on.

We make haste for Buffalo,
to grab a pint, a shot,
to chase up Dell,
his bags of powder, his bags
of pills. Bills get palmed.
Dead presidents disarrange the bar.
More purge fat lines from beef-patty boxes
junked about the walk-in-freezer.
If we hurry,
which we do,
because we can do nothing else,
we'll make Portland for last call.

At eighty-five the Roadmaster hums
a steady baseline for gypsy guitars —
guttural and lungish.

A bluefinned caddy bulls by on the right.
Davi sprawls deep and low into leather.
He fellates a soggy cigar stub,
pulls even
and flashes a hand-sign —
A-ok.

I try to sleep.

Something from the bags
is now fully operational.
Whitey's chiding eyes appear.
I open mine at once.

The caddy driver's arm,
his only arm, scours
the dash, frantic.
A Zippo flares.
A poxy face
glimmers familiar.
The caddy somehow holds a steady line.

Davi drifts right,
taps the caddy,
and straddles the center line
jubilant.
A blur pitches through gravel
snapping mileposts against chrome
as the one-armed-man's one arm
battles the wheel
until his overwrought beast lurches
back at the road beside us.

I turn away.

A bright cherry scent
inundates
the cabin of our car.

I turn back.

A Plymouth Fury
hews through the caddy's aftermath
then out and around us all.
The driver, hunched and haloed
under a bare bulb dome light, white-knuckles the wheel.

He is, I am sure,
the late great David Janssen —
once more a steadfast Dr. Richard Kimball
as I would forever have him be.

I start to speak.
Kiki rolls a bill.

Rochester Syracuse Rome Albany Troy reel by —
a moonless night deepened by gypsy guitars
and the Roadmaster's plangent clamor.
Davi breaks loose
with a keening older than words.

Kiki slithers to my lap, hisses into my ear
and translates poems I'm meant to write next week.

I might have a hard on.
I can't tell.

The Roadmaster rolls
the way I envision
the Atlantic's inexorable tides and undertow —
dread engulfing me.

I blink and swallow,
plagued by Whitey,
her eyes,
and a mind that disdains
every attempt to outrun the limits of my own.

Those Who Stay

Maybe it goes back to Marco Polo — stories
of blue-tongued camels
whose tails,
or so you were told,
change color
as sun and sky do, mutually
once more
slipping your reach.

The slick pictures in that book —
the only one the old man ever glanced at —
smelled so much stouter
than the crayon and finger-paint drawings
you made, as you imagined
painting gold
on each edge of every page
of a likewise wondrous masterpiece.

So why not Alaska —
home of the jackelope

and puffin,
the North Slope
and Kenai Peninsula.
The Spit.

Fish so big they need a bullet to the brain.

While in between,
four thousand miles of places you've never been —

Toledo
Chicago
Deadman's Gulch
Helena
Leffbridge
Banff
Bear Paw
the Yukon.

Technically, though,
it's time to gap the K car's spark plugs,
and the tire treads are worn,
and a bit unevenly at that.

Besides, there's no room for Sully's canvas —
the velvet dogs
with Vitruvian-Man bodies
parasailing above perfectly calm waters
and a perfectly replicated cursive Da Vinci.

And what about
the sixteenth hole at Whirlpool
and the all seasons
spent mastering its massive dog-leg?

All for naught?

Your outrageous bar tab?
Kirk, the canary?
And that blonde, the one
who makes those frothy coffee drinks —
the time seems right
to ask her out.

You'd need new nail scissors, too.

Oh, and that last time
your old man took you fishing,

when you actually caught something —
when that little sunny squirmed from your grip
and flopped on the bank
and bled through its gills —

the smell on your hands
kept you up all night.

Those Left Behind

Maxine had not gone on vacation —
she'd left
and left
a sign —
my toothbrush was gone
and hers had taken its place.

I used it all weekend
before it hit me,
then bought a matching Oral B.
I put hers in its old slot
and went to see what else
she'd left.

I found
nothing. No pictures or books,
no clothes in the closet,
not a sock in the dryer,
no hair in any drain.

I couldn't tell
whose scent was stranded in the sheets.

I had half a mind
to find a guy
to find whatever
files she'd missed on the Mac
but she'd taken that too.

A letter came from Baton Rouge
by way of Biloxi, I believe.
I debriefed at my bar
whose bare red bulbs
edified nicely.

The joint was empty,
no friends of hers
cracking wise and shouting rounds,

and I'd figured they'd gone too,
until I read her jibing reminder —
they'd be nowhere I might go
as they never really could
stomach the sight of me.

I read once more
as cherry blossoms dropped to the page.

I put a blossom
in my drink.

~

A postcard postmarked
Catahoula Parish
came twenty-seven weeks later.

I took it to my bar,
empty as usual.
The late November sun
warmed me some,
as I wondered where
that last, first, letter went.

I still had the toothbrush,
and I still kept the toilet seat down,
at first from habit,
then just in case,
and now
simply because
I used to do it.

Those Who Return

And off he goes, home
without another word and me
only thinking
how much shorter than I
thought I'd remembered
and older than I thought though
not gray or wrinkled,
not stooped but
flimsy —

yes —
flimsy
seems right.

He scoots by a girl
wearing a helmet,
a girl without a bike
or scooter or skateboard or skates,
which makes me think
falls or seizures.

I start
with a smart remark
to no one in particular,
about a wicker-back wheelchair,
but think, for once, twice,
and pipe down, humbled
by my own failure to thrive.

J— half-hidden behind
a crook-spined Ulysses held keenly
near squinting eyes except
when splayed face down
to make way
for forkfuls
of oversized Portuguese tart.

This same J—
sports a new 70's style shag do dyed no color I can name,
a look I wish I'd seen before.

I get up, to go across,
to say, *Hey,* only
I dread a blank stare response, or worse,
What up, in a way that signifies no notion
I'd ever left.

I quick step
the way I came
but a tricked out chopper trike
careens from Mass to Ninth
thwarting any thought to escape that way.

The driver —
or is that rider —
the guy peddling
is a guy I know
I should know,
a notorious mumbler
who mumbles something,
something about someone over there, where,
whoever she is, it seems, he says,
she needs to die.

I double-time it up the alley in his wake
and almost stumble over A—
another women
prompting hazy late-night assignations
who now rains f-bombs
on a kid
cock in hand
exercised by all the bits she's revealed
as she squats astride a steaming stream.

I know I know the poet,
boots cockeyed,
passed out amid it all,
and I remember with envy
that voice,
that talent exceeded only
by self-assured self-loathing.

Somewhere
a car alarm howls,
or it's the ice cream van,
or M—'s ring tone,
or his St. Bernard, Jinxy,
audible always, tethered, pawing
at a chicken bone
splintered in his throat.
I high-tail it any way I can.

A lime green Roadmaster rolls by right on time,
the driver's wrist bent just so over the steering wheel.
The other hand cradles a watermelon Tiparillo
punk-bright out the window.

A barista darts from patron to patron
stroboscopic in the suddenly right-turning storm.
All crush inside.

She gives me a look,
waves me in,
waits,
then bolts the lock
and disappears downstairs.

I scuffle toward the greening sky
and raise my arms to summon funnel clouds from the west.
Hail bangs off glass and steel and block
and thunder rolls in waves
but the storm peters out.

I curse,
then finger-fuck the God of Abraham
and any other idling about.

Lightning dazzles the darkened horizon,
but I remain
unremarked
dangling in the void.

Those Who Arrive

We'd met at Lizard Ball
during The Jack Lords encore
when she hipped me into a speaker
then pulled me up
passing into each palm
a silverwrapped Hershey's Kiss.

Eight days later she abandoned
her place to encroaching mold
and arrived at mine
train case in hand.

She called for coffee when up before noon —
tea at once if after one.
That hour in between
augured only uproar.

The room beneath the stairs
harbored rats and pythons
and her, forever
buffing snakeskin

or shampooing ratfur
before feeding the pups with a syringe
copped out back.

An heirloom wicker picnic basket
offered each snake a semi-private dining room
while she parsed every feed with photos, notes
and videos of every jaw unhinged,
of every melting lump —
whose sacrificial status,
known as her *elect,*
had been divined by Ouija Board.

She kept all phones off
when we were home
except during sex —
when she'd make a random call
and ask for Emma Jane,
when she'd insist
whoever it was,
was Emma Jane —
while I, watching,
as she bid, finished
my business in manual fits.

February first
she drops a horoscope in my lap:
Virgo — Split Town ASAP.

We split,
pronto,
cream soda on the counter,
for Punxsutawney, for Phil,
with a prayer the groundhog's shadow
grants six more weeks in flannel sheets.

With the backside of Paxico far behind us
she spots another Stuckey's mid-sneeze
and extracts a sacred oath —
a holy vow to the God of Misfit Toys —
that yes, yes, coming back
we'll make straight here for a Pecan Log.
The exit rolls away in the rear-view mirror.

Phil disappoints.
We flounder off
into Spring unstrung — vexed
by a sky too sharp for hope.

A blur on my left —
a silver purple gold
Hershey's Kiss-mobile blur —
it blows by at ninety, easy,
the highway patrol closing fast.

A gasp.

The sign,
the exit,
the moment,
the promise
rolling away.

The Farewells

1 ~

A fire guts the fertilizer plant just this side of Gallup.
Hydraulic ladder trucks, tankers, pumpers, EMT's
and mobile command posts clutter the tracks,
as do hoses, hydrant wrenches, air masks, axes and men.

The train hibernates
while you idle
nine hours late for Winslow —
Win-slow is how Starman,
Jeff Bridges, said it, in that movie,
though he was reunion-bound
and you newly bondfree.

You dither in the sun
and misunderstand
that sentence a sixth time.

You've been up since Wednesday.

Two blisters blister between burnt fingers
but don't dissuade you from smoking
each Pall Mall to a nub.

Caustic black smoke cascades above
a rocky high desert scrub tinged red with dust
and otherwise blooming an incandescent yellow
in your star's light.

2 ~

A cherry-lipped man in McTavish plaid —
suit coat shy one left sleeve
and Izod underneath bereft of croc —
has somehow scored shoes
that match
and an aisle seat next to you.

And why not him?

His slur and stupor
suggest he's not the chatty type,
that he might could even sleep
twenty-three-hundred-plus miles
from Show Low to Catskill —
though, in the unlikely event
that he remains
your neighbor
on another four buses, another 62 hours

(assuming the impossible occurs
and no delays ensue)
he'll need quite a stash
of cough syrup to keep him fixed,

an equitable expense
you'll gladly pay to be left
to stare at blue sky
or the back of the seat
or just rest
your head against the window
to breathe stale air,
to replay that last scene
and try to figure it out
until you figure out
there never was —
there never is —
a thing to figure out.

3 ~

The steward sings out:
Second call,
United 486 for Providence.

You slide the pass and passport
from your pocket
again
though seat 13C remains seat 13C.

He calls once more,
promising
fair skies,
kind tail winds.

You scratch your neck
then tug an ear
but do not
budge.

An urgent
almost plaintive call
for immediate and final boarding.
Someone crying whispers kissing someone else
then submits.

4 ~

The movers are late,
and you'll never find the coffee pot

(no longer even yours) in the stacked cartons
(all clusterfuck as far as you can tell)
packed (by her) wherever
she might think
a boxed up coffee pot belongs.

You dart out the door for the Greek's,
for coffee and smokes,
for a paper and box scores,
only to be waylaid by Petru,
his pushcart
and a chili cheese dog,
which reminds you,
your brother luckily won't be home
but the dog will be and it is, technically at least,
still your dog.

You pour a long something from the liquor cabinet
and plop on the couch almost on top of her.

She groans as you dig Percocets from your pocket
and fuss with the afghan she'd gathered under herself,
then she lays her head over your legs
sighing as you yank the cover
up and over
one final time.

5 ~

Her roommate's radio drones Click and Clack
through flimsy walls unfit to hold off
distraction or last night's wintery blast
when another weather service alert
warns you'll need her propane torch
to chasten that glacier entombing your car,
to get the key into the lock and crack a door
to slink inside and start the engine idling
so the heater can run
and melt the ice sheet,
so the motor warms the clutch enough
to move through gelid goo.

Your wife awaits
but this bed — warmed by a lover
whose knees melt into the back of yours,
who caresses your belly
as her own nestles glowing
into the small of your back —
shelters you as surely as
the voice which hushes you to sleep,
as the hand lighting quietly, palm upon your cheek,
letting silence arrive.

A ROUNDABOUT ROAD HOME

While I stand on the roadway, or on the pavements grey,
I hear it in the deep heart's core

> -William Butler Yeats,
> "The Lake Isle of Innisfree"

Absolute Humidity

Rain persists
as steady as the thirst swamping you since dawn —
a thirst which drives you from the train.
You end up in the Boston Public Library,
in the men's room, where,
after gulping handfuls of water,
you wring out your socks
then warm them under a hand dryer.

You try to ignore him,
but a man jerks
something from a bag.
His name, he says, is Franz, Franz Bronze.
He says he's never seen that. He starts
a camcorder and asks you to smile.

Okay?

You pass Franz later, near
the fountain outside the rare books room.
A red light blinks
as Franz points his machine —

Ahh. Exactly —

at another guy, who, posing thumbs up,
looks nothing like the bust of Mark Twain —
even the mustache is wrong.
Your feet are cold again.
They squish in your boots
which squawk across the marble floor.

Franz whispers above the whirring camera
drowning out everything except,
bathroom, socks.

The next left leads you down,
down to the lobby, where
you flit from foot to foot
while two women fill two water bottles each,
as the voice of Franz Bronze, disembodied,
floods in —
the German words,
you'd wager
if anyone cared to ask,
for careful, hurry.

Backscatter

Your hands and feet chafe
with frost
which even now kills
your overgrown roses.

This same frost
coats prickly pears
where you,
waiting for the Leonids,
lie back clutching
a scrap of agate.

You'd heard all about them ages ago
and again tonight
as you idled
through another sunset,
as drivers rubbernecked around
another outbound pileup.

No way
you'd miss them again
this time.

Meteors streak and flicker and die,
and their dying does not suit you
any more than thoughts
of your own
dying,
or even, anymore,
the memory of you
with your aggie —

knees down in dirt
shooting the taw
with a cunnythumb,
before a perfect clack
puts another Cat's Eye in your pocket.

Cyclogenesis

Sweat chills me awake.
Condensation stains
stain blankets
nailed to window frames.
Lake-effect snow leaves everything outside white
except the space between the stars.

I dress and go.
I walk at where
the sun will rise
if there is no other storm,
then turn to follow
a trail shuffling through snow.

No snow falls now —
but arctic winds still swirl —
and drifts smother all things
and confine me to the track I'm on —
halos of windblown snow dazzle
with light shone off the moon.
Snow pricks my cheeks,
my ears and nose,
my lips and tongue.

Snow drowns all sound
except the plows
and their scattershot rock salt,
except snow that shimmies against my coat.

I squint at my boots and try to hold a steady line.
Footprints fill with blown snow.
They churn through drifts
to a picnic shelter
and a man
in pinstriped jeans
who sows freshly fallen snow

by jigging a Curly Shuffle
beneath his Burger King crown.

Downburst

I nod off
at the park again today.

We'd spent less time on these swings, once
we started sleeping together.
We strayed in your car —
could have been the bugs, or the heat.
Maybe it was the promise
of flesh coupled in the tall grass prairie, or our selves
momentarily sequestered at the outskirts of towns
where no one knew us.

I tell myself all
those trips were rehearsals
for the one we'd take
each alone —
for learning to get back home, now

when unrelenting grass grows
in gravel below our swings,
and a right-turning storm
blows thunderheads in.

Exit Region

The bellhop was right.
The sun-shower turned biblical deluge.
He was right, too, about the two-bit hack —
how his cab would mist up,
how it would skim and scud across the road.

And he was right about the cooch-joint south of town.

There are no signs,
just a left-hand exit
over an inundated waste channel,
then a hurricane fence, whose cracked slats snare
the beam of our one functioning headlamp.

A building ghosts at the lowering end of a lot.

A guy at the door waves me in
like he expects me,
like he knows me.

Cigarettes smolder at the ends of cigarette holders
held by a crowd decked out in evening wear.

A waiter sidles to my table,
doles out warm mead,
wades by.
He curtsies
to a man he calls, *Herr General,*
whose head bobs politely,
whose upheld hand chokes off a fawning man
and his sales pitch pimping the Korean poodle market.
The general palms a folded bill into a waiting palm.
His right hand slips field glasses from a sack.

Orange blossoms —
and sweat and whiskey and musk —
waft from the stage and over Herr General,
his binoculars and his man —

orange blossoms sweat whiskey musk
languishing around me —
the way shale flakes skipped across a stream
drift into muck.

Friction

54 highway.

I coast, broken down,
to its crumbling shoulder, just inside the Kansas line.
Fetid Texas feed lots hover in the overheated car.

Sweat and humidity seep
through a postcard of Hooker, Oklahoma
and blot the blurb of a Depression-era downtown.

I'm not sure where the birds might be
but guess the bugs have burrowed
away from the sun,
a sun that's fused,
to every breath of air inhaled,
some rank particulate cast off
by the multi-state void called The Plains.

A tandem axle dump truck grinds by,
its bucket bursting with rubble —
its wake of dust swarms my car
and reanimates that feculent bovine stink.

I flip the card and scratch
my name in its *To* box,
above General Mail
Beatrice, Nebraska —
where I'll fetch it,
next time I lose my way.

Ground Clutter

A burnt-out chimney
for sale aside 52 Highway
just this side of Bowbells, North Dakota
where the temperature drops
faster than the dying
dusk sun.

A Black backed Woodpecker scolds from a bale of hay.
Acres of sunflowers, brown, bent, heads low.

You've got maybe just enough coffee.
The road is new and smooth and black
like the obsidian splinter in your pocket.

The prairie and power lines,
the plateau and barbed wire
yield to a Pleistocene river bed —

and you'd like to know —

has duck season begun?
Are the missile silos nearby?

Heat Index

Bus diesel overwhelms
the taste of sweat on my tongue.
Tar melts into my shoes.
Ocotillos pack up and head for the shade.

This is no day for wingtips and a tie.

Our bed was like this
every winter enduring
a dozen blankets under a sleeping bag —
warming up, you warn, for tropical nights.

A Gremlin sputters by,
its engine blazing from the hood.
A family of six spills out
then hacks at flames
with newspapers, rain gear, a straw hat.

I knew Panama
only through dreams
you drew — downy beaches
beneath a molten melon sky.

An old man fans himself.
His inked up racing form
keeps the beat for bare inked up feet
tapping the time
of time to kill.

You cooked with chipotle,
lime and cilantro, with habanero —
sweat purled between your breasts,
around your navel.
The small of your back
trembled, slick,
fluent to my touch.

Two women skip out a door
then down the porch steps.
They squat at the curb and crack an egg.

I straighten my tie
and wipe my brow
and pocket a pickeystone
from a hopscotch square.

Instability

Another late-season loss,
and the heat above ninety
like the year you turned twelve
when they left Briggs Stadium behind for the year —
and eleven games in nine days,
and another second division season
that ended mercifully soon enough,
unlike those triple digit temperatures in Detroit, again,
and it's September, for the love of Pete.

Even the rookie, that kid Kaline,
had wilted and barely hit his weight.
The bonus baby flop.

You unplug the radio
to run the fan over a block of dry ice
you'd meant to hew into chunks.
The root cellar sits empty,
the icepick dull,
and mallet missing,
and your head swims
with the fan's touch-and-go wheeze.

You swelter sweating,
or maybe it's just this humidity.
Your leather gloves, your leather apron,
reek of something dank.
Your steamer trunk of surplus Vaudeville costumes
fares no better beneath the steps and out of sight.

How long can it last?

You dry hands that sweat,
and the concertina —
the one Uncle Bardhosh brought
when he fled Apollonia.
A *kaba*, the way he played,
is the only thing for a night like this,
but you'd never asked him how,
and nobody left knows what one is.

A polka will do just as well,
or maybe a waltz.

The refrigerator groans,
and you wish you'd called the electrician back.

You lift a runestone paperweight
and grab at sheet music.

You'd start in,
but something's off, you think,
or maybe it's the damp air, or your vision
of Kaline's slumping cowlick, which always seems
twinned to heat like this.

You wipe the instrument down,
stash it away,
make a note to have it cleaned.
You turn to the typewriter —
Corona No. 4 — from the hock shop
near your father's office at the Free Press.
Hemingway used this one too.
Yours is maroon,
built in '25, when Cobb got his save —
his penultimate season here.

You're thinking short stories.
No, a novel, a roman a clef —
House Peepers and Pugs on the Homefront.

You feed the paper, adjust the ribbon.

Sweat stipples the title page.
You wipe.
You squint.
Tap.

H might could use a spot of oil.
Could be the Shift key.

You lean for a closer look.
A fuse blows —
all goes dark.

January Thaw

A car horn
loud long
insistent
just as suddenly gone

jolts you to the window —
open because you can't control the heat,
because the radiator works its own will.
A shovel clangs against cement
five floors down.
It chops and scrapes at ice.
Ice slung across the shovel pan
cracks against an ice-packed snowbank.

A woman
calls her Papi,
who
if he hears,
if he's out there at all
shows no will to respond.

Tea? you say,
to yourself
who then replies, *Tea, indeed!*

The kettle heats
too slow for you, but quick
as any hot plate gets it done.

Woolen wet flakes
widely fall, softly, as you
finger the blob of blue howlite
you'd long ago thought you'd lost —
though just now found, abiding alone
once the last tea bag
dropped out the casket.
The whistle blows
as snowflakes
at the street
morph to sleet to slush,
which, you know,
as is its wont
reverts to ice
when it will.

K Index

I'm in the bathroom
most mornings
all morning —
the only place
I escape her sorrow. Sometimes,

I stare at the mirror,
but mostly, I need
to catch my breath,
let dank porcelain
soothe my sunburned back.

The sink pedestal
and soapstone floor tiles offer
no relief —
the tub and shower wall
likewise disappoint —
but toilet tank condensate
in the power of its healing ablutions
is surpassed only by tears
from a Blessed Virgin Statuette.

My eye in the mirror stares back.
The furrows and folds of my iris sink
deeper, the meshwork echoes
darker than the hour before
or the day — or whenever
I last tore myself
away.

A black border bounds the iris
and blurs into almost blue.
I find no definition.

The pupil contracts
as sunlight flares through the window —
it dilates when clouds
tremble by
hushed as a sob.

I find a man, staring
from that hole, mute
but no way else
like me.

Latent Heat

A whimper —
the cat,
something, someone
in here, her, somewhere
back in the bedroom —
my eye opens.

I close it — still
a moan
or dream
or phantom keen recurs —
and the eye opens again.

It scans the room and finds
nothing but silhouettes
blooming almost incarnate
in a red aura emanating
from the pomegranate night light
she'd flung at that very same eye.

The dog whines at the door.

I squeeze my eye shut, afraid
they're all awake.

I get up, go out,
try to find Alpha Cygni in the east,
where you, and the star map
you gave me, said it would be —

Wait. A little
that way.
There. Mars. Now
Cygnus.

You'll be a mile underground,
in a gold mine across the world, with the sun
and Spring waiting.

I find a rag in the shed
and shine the red jasper spheres
sinking into the wreck of my hyacinth.
I put the rag back
and bring my telescope out,
and sit naked under an Indian Summer sky,
and track the swan
through all this dark.

Mackerel Sky

A sun ablaze bores
from the horizon, seething
through motel drapes as frayed as clouds
throwing no shade to the brokedown road grader
or dead orange orchards
as grass fires haunt all hope for sleep,
and the penny for your thoughts drowns in molten tar.

The air conditioner does not now blow cold,
has never blown cold,
and seems, like you, disinclined to change.

You need smokes, and something,
anything, to drink, if you can
face that girl —
the one with one freckle inside an ear —
whose eyes dart from yours, who fidgets
with something behind her back
as you mutter into the void —

The Marlboros...
The green ones...
The menthols...

No, the green ones.
The Marlboro menthols. Right there. Those.

And as to the couple next door,
at it once more all day, as at it all day every day
just for you, you're sure —

Oh Mommy, so hot, too hot Mommy!

— their post-coital refraction is worse —
the silence simply prelude
anticipating another incestuous climax.

You're tempted by the neon promise of *Chilled Air*
wheezing behind that girl at the lobby counter,
but guests like you —
or let's be honest here, you —
rank as loiterers, and are, as such,
as the sign instructs, STRICTLY FORBIDDEN!

The copper-rocked mesa juts up more jagged
under a turquoise sky turning black.

The red clay road goads
with a more urgent orange at dusk.

Back home, when
you had a home —
beyond all that sandstone,
down this same road
long after the rubberized asphalt starts —
you'd be settling into a pitcher of whiskey sours
while patio misters drizzle cooling mist
and a rasping voice sings, *Arrorró mi niño* —
audible above broken tailpipes and thumping subwoofers
and a belly-dumper's whinging brakes,
while Orion rises calm above palms
and helicopter searchlights —
much like it will rise tonight, here, above all
those scorpions scrambling from bulldozed citrus.

Nephelococcygia

That rain.

I got
knuckles big as chestnuts. Look.

Give us a reason
to be here,
though, right?
I mean, why I'm here.
You, well you,
you got to work.
Except for rain
I won't normally do gin this early,
you know that,
not like some
I could name.

Right?

I was here earlier, too
but you was late.

Only I was craving
that egg salad in my fridge,
which I told you about last night
or might've been last Tuesday
when the storm come on.

So anyhow, I start
home, but it's like this,
see, my neighbor,
I told you about him.
No?
Don't matter.

He jumps out
in some kind of man-kini-mini-dick-thong-thing,
starts mowing his lawn
sloshing his push-mower through skeeters and crabgrass
sprouting up between the slate pavers I gave him
that my old man was supposed to build us a patio with
before he beat it with that, that…

well I ain't got to tell you.

And I know he been after me
ever since, and now him

slipping around them stones
in that downpour
and all his junk
might as well been out for everyone to see,
'cept far as I can see
they ain't really nothing much to see.

He start waving,
so I'm thinking I know
and make I got a call —
you know, pull out the phone,
put it to my ear and all,
but then,
of course,
that fool thing ring for real.

The ex, who else, right?
Who's short on alimony
and child support
and maybe we should
revisit things —
revisit,
that's how he say it —

but what really gets me is
the whole time
that man keep pawing himself
like he got some rash down there
and watching me with that look they give you.
You know.
You see it, too.

Anyway,
I lost my appetite
and just come back here
for a gin or two,
though, maybe a double E & J might be more like it
if you could get me that tab goin' again.

It's all too much.
I mean, who can take it,

all this rain?

Occluded Front

I am sick, today.
My head congested. Feverish.
The wind. I hear it all day.
Alberta Clipper. That's what they call it.

It knows no remorse.

I only know how it beats the panes
and gushes from the baseboards
through gaps I've meant to seal.

My pills, they tranquilize and agitate
and I nod off and wake,
nod off,
then wake as chunks of ice crack off the roof
and crash against limestone blocks
bulging from the foundation wall.

This pink patch on my quilt
is a pink I know from you,
is the pink of your chicken-pox,
the pink of the lotion

I used to soothe you —
from the part of your hair to your baby-toe.

Everything ends like it begins,
and you have one pockmark left —
more dimple than scar —
a spot that calls for a kiss.

The last time we talked,
we talked because the dog had died.
She was, you'd said,
the last bond between us.

I said nothing. You said how
awkward it was
to tell me
about this new guy,
this What's-His-Name —
I tried to sound surprised
and kind.

I'd like to believe
I'll lie to you no more.

Prefrontal Trough

Just one spot open,
next to a woman you didn't know,
who wasn't a regular, yet.

You sat quietly
aware her fluid dynamics
text, open on the bar, imposed
a clue
too big to miss.

Bud poured a rye whiskey,
then poured another.

Keith blubbered to the woman,
the only one here
apparently,
who hadn't already heard his tale of woe:
his hard-hearted ex, the back rent she ducked out on,
and his poor old mum — two years gone,
today being the day she died,
and yet, and still,
no marker,

because his old lady, who'd said she'd pay,
sits all day, here, awash in cognac,
and he'd designed the headstone himself, and had it cut —
pink granite with a carving of St. Jude, and some birds,
because how much his mother loved birds —
and wasn't that sad, Mum,
out there anonymous
and alone.

No tale like that gets anyone laid,
as he'd found out
when she'd turned to me
to ask something about sloe gin,
which was funny, in a kismet kind of way,
because I had a story about it, sloe gin, that is,
though it wasn't much of a story,
but what the hell,
at least nobody died.

And now we've got a sloe gin story,
one that has no climax, yet,
and won't until one of us dies — an ending
I might consider sad if I didn't believe
that Keith's story only works as farce
because it's too sad
to tell any other way.

Quality of Snow

You're at the door, looking
past her, looking through
the blinds
into all that sky
on the first warm day of almost Spring
when you can wander around
the grounds in shorts
or pajamas and a robe.

The aide says, again —
Boots instead of slippers, honey,
not over them.

"Jailhouse Rock,"
Montovani style dripping with strings,
mews somewhere in the corridor behind you.

She smiles flatly
at the aide, or you —

She tilts her head
and touches a cheek.

All the paths are clear and dry,
so you carry her stick
keeping your arm looped through hers.
She pats your wrist when you move too fast.

Sunlight bangs off melting snow
and her diamond ring.

Elvis — she says —
Elvis was a gentleman.
Did I ever tell you the time...

but geese, returning
home above you,
honk,
and honk.

Radial Velocity

I go to Chuckie
because he cuts my hair
the way I want it cut.
He's quick. And cheap and always open,
and old men with phlegmy croaking throats
engulf his shop.

I go because everybody's Baby.
Hey, Baby. How you doing, Baby?
Baby, grab a seat.

Today, Chuckie says, *Wait.*
He's in the chair,
hair on top of his head brushed straight up —
the sides sprayed stiff out like...
like hair shelves.

A blow dryer whines from his clutched right hand
while his bald spot
foams under blueblack aerosol spray.
He spins around, pops up, waves me over
and cinches me into an apron.

I hear scissors snip
then go still.
Snip and go still.

Chuckie starts in on taxes, the crooks at city hall,
and those damn Mets — again this year.
He jabs the point end of a comb.

He's had enough of them all,
and those knee-deep potholes out front.
And what do I think?

And I think, Hey, Baby,
I'm only here for a haircut,
so watch the eyes.

But I just kind of nod.

Something hisses
and an oily film coats my ears.
Chuckie buzzes the clippers a bit.
They quit.
He clicks and clicks and clicks the switch
then yanks the cord from the wall.

He sprays a spare, buzzes, clicks them off.

It's the ex, see.
She's a little short this month,
something about the furnace
and fire insurance,
like I ain't got issues.
You get me, Baby?
And listen here, now, the boy —
what's he, eight —
and already gone and busted up his knuckles
on some fool teacher's head.
I mean, Baby, what is that shit?

My head jerks back
as Chuckie yanks through a knotted curl.
He rakes the comb out
and launches it ninja-style
at a beaker of blue fluid.

He thwaps a straight razor across a strop,
then scourges a whetstone with it.

So now the landlord's jacked the rent
because times are tougher than they was in the day.

As if Chuckie don't know times is tough!
As if Chuckie don't know the day!

I'm telling you Baby,
I been sweeping other folks's mess near on thirty-five years,
while that God-damned squire and his half-bastard son
too cheap to pay for a shave.

Not a hair on my head's been cut.
Not one whisker clipped.

Chuckie brushes the back of my neck and wipes my face.
He spins the barber chair at the mirror.
He shakes a bottle and pats my neck,
and a cloud of talc
obscures our reflection.

I'm telling you, Baby,
even the garlic in my garden's gone to shit.

Sun Dog

A violent violet horizon crowns
Squaw Peak, which hulks agleam
more green than it should be,
as cactus pollen teeming in my head
nibbles at my eyes,
as it has all night,

like the night the power went out
(the a.c. and fridge with it)
because I forgot the bill,
and we lay in the hammock and made up
new constellations from stars rising
beyond that jagged mass of hill,
or mountain,
or whatever it actually is.

Traffic grinds beyond my cinder block wall.
Day-lilies, in the box of yard the wall makes,
beg for water and someone
to deadhead the petals
withered by a desert sun
relentlessly doing as it does,

like scorch your overgrown eggplants
or wither the night blooming jasmine
into a brittle snarl of knots.

Your scent was that scent —
Floris — wafting around me
even as you turned away
to slip something
into the makeup-counter labcoat pocket.

An indigo lip print smudged your left lapel.

~

I never knew
you had an iron
until I saw you in your suit,
packed for the bus back east
with so many bags — and yet, nothing
seemed amiss
when I went back in.

My car succumbs to the sun's radiant heat
enflamed by this brown smog haze. Claustrophobic
I grub for change in the void
beneath the seats,

then with my quarter
scrounge around outside, here,
among Quonset huts anchoring
a grid of roads and rectangular lots,
until I find a blue and yellow pay phone
whose handset, once I grab it,
burns and brands my palm.

~

The guy at the wheel of the tow-truck
unties the bandana atop a balding head.
He folds it precisely, mops his ruddy face and neck.
His image barks from the side-view mirror —
did I check the gas?

I had not,
so say nothing
when I climb in — stunned
as purple sparks
ignited by sunlight
and rhinestones on a dangling garter
erupt across the wrecker's cab,
itself burnt by twilight,
an alien, ecstatic orange.

Towering Cumulus

Clouds above your bench
collide, while
the Rock of Ages
jabs the sole of a foot
crammed inside your too-tight boot.

You find no will to dig it out.

A black cat stalks a crow
strutting across a patch of grass.

The mailman's step van slow rolls by,
as does a dog in the sidecar
of a girl pedaling hard upwind.

Boys carve by on longboards, silent
except for well-greased bearings
and polyurethane wheels.

The man who limps
scolds the wife who doesn't.

A skunk scuttles from under a dumpster,
through a bar door left ajar.
Tweakers flee.

Contrails
or clouds dissolve
the edge of white and blue.

Someone whispers your name
you think — maybe
it's that crow
or another skunk.

You wait,
hands clamped to your bench, sure
you hear your name
louder.
Softer.
Quavering.

Your calves cramp.
You've bitten your cheek.

You find no crow or cat.
No skater punks.

No bike, skunk, clouds, limp or wife.

The foot benumbed,
with boot, fades away.

No Rock is
or ever was,

and if that was your name before,
it is no
more.

U Burst

The beer bottle bird —
she'd said when the monsoons hit —
is made for the rains but each dry season
eats sand to survive.
The female leaves. It sleeps
alone in a soffit or galvanized
pipe of a chain link fence.
The male waits by the blossom
of a peach tree's new shoot.
He girds the nest with empty beer bottles.
He blows across them,
two long low notes.

Wind and rain stung
the house that night, the night
she threw another flagstone through the window.
You'd just finished rinsing
a pair of chick peas
from her plate
and jumped at the crash.

She never came home —
not even once
the skies had cleared,

not after you scraped and painted your house,
hung empty bottles of every kind
from railings, gutters, eaves
and the dying tree's limb.

You smoke on the stoop
each night, until the sonorous traffic fades —

nothing blooms,
there are no birds,
not a breath of a breeze
to make those bottles sing —
there's only absence —
a vacuum filled by earnest voices —

Is it a love song,
you ask —

No,
she says, *No.*

*There is no love
song.*

Virga

A whiff of stale
stagnant air —
the only breeze about —
stirs only when the bus
chugs between stops.

A guy swabs
a patchily shaved head
with a tattered laced hanky.

No.
That'd be an antimacassar.

He unzips
a bowling ball bag,
pulls out a ukulele,
strums where strings should be.

The bus stops.
The air stops.

A woman in flannel pajamas
swipes her pass.

Slippers
spank her heels
and scuff across the aisle.

The next stop is you.

The next stop is Rosa —
tinged red in a tail-light glow —
rolling deodorant under each arm.

The next stop is cigarette embers
dotting the stoops of brownstone row houses,

your own flat
and the reek of bananas,

and echoes from upstairs —
Dolores,
her television,
the evening news,
the weatherman
who says,

More of the same.
No break in the foreseeable future.

Wet Bulb Depression

Scorched by the midsummer sun,
your van's panels scald bare skin,
even in the evening,
even on the inside
where air withers
desperate to be refreshed
among spare parts and oily tools.

One late last job
interrupts your growler of beer
and the final edition's baseball news —
both will wait at home out back
as substitute for sleep
in heat you take as retribution
for every wayward act.

White noise whirs from the swamp cooler —
the tang of booze, smokes, grease
sex and unwashed flesh —

broken linoleum
and blood-tinged bangers jabbed in plaster —

23B — the peep hole painted over, again —
the door jamb cracked where the deadbolt goes.
A carpet remnant, frayed at the edges but swept clean.

The woman who always answers
does as expected.
The gash slants from eyebrow to ear lobe.
The bruise abloom across her punctured cheek.
A rasping snore gasps in, chokes out.

You slip out of your boots
as she whispers
about a bus,
crashing down the street
last night, so bad
it smashed the window.

You say nothing
about that,
about her turtleneck shirt,
about the glass shards strewn outside,
or the pane's head-shaped hole.

X-Rays

The kid in the flat
behind you wails through the wall while up
the street the panel beater's burglar alarm
howls with equal fervor
and equal likelihood of ending
no time soon.

The bells of St. Whoever
and your own internal echo
indicate the toddler is
a tick early tonight,
the red alert a tad late.

A tomcat scores the arm
of an armchair moldering on the porch,
pisses into the stuffing he's unstuffed,
bounds down, then up
at your window's Perspex
until assured its paw-sized aperture allows no ingress —
and so the skirling starts.

You flip your pillow
to find the new side just as lumpy.

The moon,
waxing or waning,
(and who can keep that straight?)
sheds more light than the bare globe strung from a wire
in this crypt the rental agent calls, *Your rooms.*
Neither moon nor globe illuminates
enough to read by,
but, as this is New Zealand,
one should take solace from the fact
that both are energy efficient —
though even absent flicker and hum
a low-watt fluorescent tube coiled to mimic a globe
displeases myriad ways,
as does the moldy-silled window —

however one might still,
contrary to your yowling cat companion,
rest assured after being told
no poisonous jumping spiders,
no venomous snakes loom here,
waiting to creep through
where flywire screens ought be —

and you squirm unconsoled, anyway, as nothing holds
back mosquitoes and blow flies whose droning
complacency unsettles so much more
than those phobias
or the noises you want to blame
for your own
unquiet insomnia.

Yellow Wind

That Christmas Eve I skipped
around wearing our Christmas stockings
my parents made me
sit on the couch and read
while the rest of them trimmed the tree.

The book was *Uncle Wiggily,*
about a rheumatic rabbit with a balloon
which sailed him around the world
and straight into the shit —

a balloon — like the fantastical skilligimink,
a made up color of a made up word —
that let me hope
I might escape Akron a while.

~

Mrs. Pierce was not the first
teacher to move me
from the trouble I caused,

consigning me and my desk
to each corner of the room
and then right beside her own desk,
but she succumbed
to failure best —
Bring a book, she said. *Read,*
take the tests, shut up, that's all.
Please.

I got through *Hot Corner Blues* and *Papillon,*
The Count of Monte Christo, all of Tolkien,
and 8th grade.

~

The first woman
I found to love me, read me
random poems in bed,
but troubles
followed just the same,

like they do
now, here
on a balcony

up against the outskirts of Quemado
where I scribble marginalia
through a Gideons Bible
until reddish particulates —
in a hue I know
as Ohio Cupboard Rust —
blow in from, let's say, the rodeo grounds,
or maybe from the calcified lake
and bluffs just beyond Omega —
they stain the canopy of Bianca's Last Stop Lodge,
vex my arms and legs,
and leave dull footprints inside
where I go to call the old man
and tell them I might make it
there, home, sometime
soon.

Zastrugi

After mittfulls of mushrooms
the golf course becomes tundra
crowned with frozen white waves
whose ice crusts crack as you clomp around,
as the dog sprints along,
sprints and skids
and stops and sniffs and starts.
You follow her blurred blue merle trails
as ice crystals flicker across all this whiteness.

You love that dog.

You've loved her
since you brought her home —
when she curled up by your feet,
then slept by your chair,
and wouldn't budge for food,
for water,
to do her business,
until the morning,
when you came down
to ask how she liked it here.

You come to a boulder
that has no business
in this or any other fairway.
You sit in the snow,
lean back,
watch her wander off,
as she does. As she did
in the wetlands
when she found the muskrat carcass,
as she did at Christopher Creek
when she first heard trumpeting elk.

Cold settles
on, in, all around you.

She's looked after you
as much as you have her,
like the time she lunged
at some drunk's crotch
and came away with a mouthful of shorts —
or the time in Portsmouth
when that self-proclaimed dog-whisperer
wouldn't fuck off, as you'd advised,
and she sprang and snapped
just scratching his jugular.

And each time, you said nothing,
just rubbed her chest once they'd gone.

You stretch through a yawn
as the wind picks up.

Portsmouth was after Utica, after Cayuga Lake,
after Buffalo, Columbus, Lawrence and Phoenix.

Before York,
before Acadia and back to York,
before Buffalo, Indy, Lawrence,
Arches, Canyonlands, the North Rim
and back to Lawrence.
Ten weeks in the truck,
both of you stinking like dead fish.

Just one last trip, you'd thought.

But instead off to Auckland
where she followed half a year later,
greeted by you and a month of quarantine,
then soon back here
again, once
Plans A through E flashed a cold shoulder.

She got back a week after you,
and, leaning against her crate,
ignored each Hiya, every Atta girl,
until, hackles raised, she turned
and glared, scowling,
as if to ask if you were done.

Stars fade
behind a fog of breath.

She crouches beside you, snarls then barks —
It's cold,
we want to go home.

Ed Tato lives in Seaford, Australia with his wife and daughter. His poems abide in various books, print journals and websites. They wait—painted under the floorboards of a bedroom in Lawrence, Kansas—crumpled by the toilet on the bus from Eureka to El Dorado—for someone, anyone, to find, to read, to pause and say, yes, that's about right, I kind of thought that, too.

www.ingramcontent.com/pod-product-compliance
Lightning Source LLC
Chambersburg PA
CBHW030331100526
44592CB00010B/654